BBC Gardeners' World

POCKET PLANTS

SHRUB ROSES

Andi Clevely

Photographs by Jo Whitworth

BBC Books

Author Biography

Andi Clevely has been a working gardener for nearly thirty years. He began his career in Leeds City Council central nurseries and since then has worked in many gardens around the country, including Windsor Great Park. He is now responsible for a country estate and large garden in Stratford-on-Avon where he lives with his wife. Andi has written a number of gardening books and is a regular columnist for *Homes & Gardens* magazine.

Acknowledgements

The publishers would like to thank David Austin Roses; Royal National Rose Society, St Albans; Mattocks Roses, Oxfordshire and Apuldram Roses, Chichester for their assistance with the photography. All photographs © BBC.

More Information

If you have difficulty finding any of the roses listed in this book contact The Royal National Rose Society, The Gardens of the Rose, Chiswell Green, St Albans, Hertfordshire, AL2 3NR (01727) 850461.

Published by BBC Books,
an imprint of BBC Worldwide Publishing.
BBC Worldwide Limited, Woodlands,
80 Wood Lane, London W12 0TT.

First published 1997
© BBC Worldwide Limited 1997
The moral right of the author has been asserted

ISBN 0 563 38776 9

Photographs by Jo Whitworth

Set in Futura

Printed and bound in Belgium by Proost NV
Colour separations by Radstock Reproductions Limited, Midsomer Norton, Avon
Cover printed in Belgium by Proost NV

Finding the Rose for Your Garden

 Award-winning roses

 Good disease resistance

 Strong fragrance

Award-winning roses		Good disease resistance		Strong fragrance	
Ballerina	10	Abraham Darby	6	Abraham Darby	6
Bonica	11	A Shropshire Lad	9	Charles Austin	16
Buff Beauty	13	Candy Rose	14	Cornelia	17
Cornelia	17	Cornelia	17	Cymbeline	19
Felicia	27	Cymbeline	19	Eglantyne	21
Flower Carpet	29	Fair Bianca	26	Evelyn	25
Fred Loads	33	Felicia	27	Fair Bianca	26
Golden Wings	35	Flower Carpet	29	Felicia	27
Graham Thomas	36	Fountain	30	Francesca	31
Many Happy Returns	50	Francesca	31	Glamis Castle	34
Marguerite Hilling	51	Francine Austin	32	Grouse	37
Mountbatten	57	Fred Loads	33	Heather Austin	38
Nevada	58	Golden Wings	35	Heavenly Rosalind	39
Nozomi	60	Graham Thomas	36	Heritage	40
Penelope	64	Grouse	37	Hilda Murrell	41
Rosy Cushion	67	Heather Austin	38	Jacquenetta	43
Sally Holmes	69	Heavenly Rosalind	39	Jude the Obscure	45
Scharlachglut	71	Heritage	40	Leander	48
Suma	73	Jacqueline du Pré	42	Lucetta	49
Surrey	74	Jacquenetta	43	Many Happy Returns	50
Yesterday	80	John Clare	44	Mary Rose	52
		L D Braithwaite	47	Mistress Quickly	53
		Leander	48	Moonlight	55
		Lucetta	49	Noble Antony	59
		Many Happy Returns	50	Nur Mahal	61
		Mary Rose	52	Nymphenburg	62
		Mistress Quickly	53	Penelope	64
		Morning Mist	56	Snow Goose	72
		Mountbatten	57	St Swithun	68
		Noble Antony	59	Scepter'd Isle	70
		Nur Mahal	61	Sweet Juliet	76
		Pink Bells	65	The Dark Lady	77
		Red Blanket	66	Tradescant	78
		Rosy Cushion	67		
		St Swithun	68		
		Scepter'd Isle	70		
		Snow Goose	72		
		Tradescant	78		

INTRODUCTION

Summer means roses, especially fragrant shrub roses tumbling all over the border and shedding carpets of petals. There is a wide mixture of varieties generally classified as shrub roses, and they all bring beauty into the garden.

This book concentrates mainly on modern shrub roses. The shape of their flowers is very appealing, sometimes classically simple but often fat and full of petals, bending the branches under the weight of blooms and providing great quantities for cutting and filling bowls. Many modern hybrids flower almost continuously all summer, and sometimes well into autumn. Most are also intensely fragrant, with scents ranging from heavy and seductive to bracingly fruity. Some have marked disease-resistance, and also an ability to tolerate a wide range of soils and situations, so that they can be grown in gardens that might not suit more conventional roses. (The particular qualities and disease resistance of each rose are listed later.)

Shrub roses vary in form from large strong shrubs to the prostrate varieties that spread across large areas, and can be grown as low-maintenance ground cover. Some resemble wild roses in the simplicity of their gracefully arching stems, while others are sometimes classified as floribundas because of their massed displays of small flowers in large sprays. The great diversity of this exciting group means that there is an ideal rose for almost any situation.

Siting Shrub Roses

Because of their unusual beauty, shrub roses deserve prominent positions. They can be planted in special rose beds and borders very successfully, but often look more delightful when treated like any other shrub and planted in existing flower beds as single specimens, or in small groups of three for maximum impact where there is space.

They are versatile plants, too. Upright varieties can be grown as flowering hedges or even in large containers, while a ground cover type may be trained against a fence or wall as though it were a restrained climber. Some of the taller, more vigorous shrubs ('Nevada' and 'Marguerite Hilling', for example) are also eye-catching when trained flat on a wall or fence.

Some flower best in full sun or very fertile soil, but most tolerate a variety of situations. They do not like heavy shade or competition from other more vigorous shrubs though, and like all varieties they will not do well on the same spot where roses previously grew, unless the exhausted soil is dug out and replaced with fresh soil from elsewhere in the garden.

Preparing the ground

Deep cultivation and manuring before planting improves the health and performance of all roses, so dig the site deeply, removing perennial weeds (especially where ground cover roses are to be grown) and working in a generous quantity of well-rotted manure or garden compost, if possible at least a bucketful to every square metre (yard) of ground. If there is time, do this a month or two before planting to allow the soil a chance to settle.

Planting

Late autumn and early winter, while the bushes are dormant, are the best times to plant bare-root or container-grown roses — later plants need great care with watering during the following season, especially on light soils, and may not grow so vigorously at first.

Plant roses ordered from a nursery as soon as they arrive. In frosty weather they can be left in their packaging for a few days, but if planting is still impossible after this, heel them in temporarily outdoors by digging a hole large enough to bury their roots and firming them in.

- Before planting, trim off any damaged roots and then stand the plants in a bucket of water for an hour or two.

- Dig a hole large enough to accommodate all the roots comfortably and without cramping them.

- Position the plant in the hole so that the graft union (the knobbly joint where the branches meet the stem) is just above ground level.

- Filter soil between the roots, lightly shaking this into place and firm gently.

- Replace the rest of the soil in 2–3 stages, treading it firm each time, and level the surface.

Care

Watering: Roses planted after late winter should be watered in thoroughly immediately afterwards, and again every 2–3 weeks until they are growing vigorously. Once established, roses should not need watering, especially if mulched in spring.

Feeding: Mulching feeds roses and also reduces water loss. Mulch moist soil in mid-autumn or mid-spring with well-rotted manure, garden compost, leafmould or grass clippings from lawns untreated with herbicide. Most roses benefit from a feed of powdered or granular rose fertilizer in spring, with a further application in mid-summer for heavy-flowering varieties.

Pruning: There is no need to prune shrub roses during their first season or two, while they are building up a framework of branches. Thereafter prune in winter by first cutting out dead and diseased wood, and any weak sideshoots. One or two of the oldest branches can be removed annually from mature bushes to stimulate new growth and leave room for young stems to develop.

For large plants and masses of smaller blooms, you can leave the remaining branches untouched or merely lightly tipped. For more compact bushes and fewer, larger blooms, shorten the branches by one-third to one-half. There are no hard and fast rules: you can usually prune as little or as much as you choose, and some varieties can be pruned in a number of different ways. It is worth experimenting if a particular shrub suggests a certain shape, because shrub roses are noted for being adaptable and forgiving plants.

Health care: Clear away all fallen leaves in autumn and burn them. Many shrub roses are very healthy, but others may be prone to mildew, black spot or rust, and these should be sprayed to prevent problems occurring. (See information under individual plants.) Aphids are fond of roses, and although small numbers are rarely troublesome, you should use a systemic insecticide if infestations become serious.

Abraham Darby

Shapely bushy growth combined with the old-fashioned appearance of the cup-shaped blooms makes this a desirable rose for varied sites. The flowers are particularly showy, with a rich fruity scent.

Season: Repeatedly throughout summer.

Foliage: Bright, shiny and rich green.

Height: 1.5m (5ft)

Spread: 1.5–2.4m (5–8ft)

Soil: Well-drained and fertile.

Positioning: Full sun; excellent for a wide border or shrubbery; also succeeds on a fence or wall.

Care: Benefits from plenty of well-rotted manure in autumn, and a good mulch of compost in late spring.

Pruning: From second year onwards, shorten strong stems by one-third to one-half in winter to keep bushes compact, or trim lightly and leave to spread to full size.

Useful tips: May also be grown as a climber on walls and fences: leave unpruned for first 2–3 years, then thin aging surplus stems and shorten flowered side-shoots to 8cm (3in) long.

Angelina

Season: Repeat flowering until early autumn.

Foliage: Light green and healthy.

Height: 105cm (3½ft)

Spread: 105cm (3½ft)

Soil: Any well-drained fertile soil.

Positioning: Full sun or light shade; as specimens or groups at the front of a border or as edging for a shrubbery.

Care: Undemanding. Manure in autumn and mulch in spring.

Pruning: Remove weak and dead growth in winter or spring, and trim lightly to shape with shears. Plants are naturally shapely and well-branched. It is often more important to thin the growth to permit good air circulation than to shorten stems by very much.

Useful tips: The neat compact growth makes this a good candidate for informal hedges: plant 45–60cm (18–24in) apart in single or double staggered rows, and prune to shape late each winter.

A modern cultivar with an unusually neat and rounded shape, small enough to be used in semi-formal positions. Its prominent stamens are attractively displayed by the semi-double blooms, carried in trusses that appear regularly during the season.

Armada

One of its parents is 'New Dawn', so a memorable display is guaranteed. The semi-double flowers are almost hybrid tea in shape as buds unfurl, but these open to produce trusses of rich pink flattened blooms on very upright stems.

Season: Repeat flowering summer and autumn.
Foliage: Bright green and shiny.
Height: 1.35–1.5m (4½–5ft)
Spread: 75–90cm (2½–3ft)
Soil: Rich and well-cultivated.
Positioning: Full sun only; in borders, trained on a pillar or in containers.
Care: Good growing conditions are essential, so prepare the ground lavishly before planting; mulch annually in autumn with decayed manure and in spring with compost after feeding; feed again at mid-summer.
Pruning: Remove dead and diseased wood in winter, shorten taller stems and remove a few older ones each year to encourage new basal shoots. The habit is naturally high, and pruning should emphasize this.
Useful tips: May be trained against a pillar by thinning the stems to leave a few of the strongest and tallest for tying in, shortening one or two others to bear the lower blooms.

A Shropshire Lad

Season:	Repeat flowering all summer.
Foliage:	Dark green, neat and shiny.
Height:	1.2m (4ft) or more
Spread:	90cm (3ft) or more
Soil:	Fertile and well-cultivated, but tolerates poorer soils.
Positioning:	Full sun or light shade; in groups in beds and borders, especially towards the back, and as large specimen bushes.
Care:	Mulch with garden compost in spring, and feed in spring and mid-summer; on lighter soils manure well in autumn.
Pruning:	Remove dead wood in winter, plus some of the older stems; shorten young growth by half to maintain size and vigour. For larger bushes prune less severely in spring.
Useful tips:	One of the larger 'English Roses', making a quite substantial bush if pruned lightly, although repeat flowering may not then be so impressive.

A practical and particularly disease-resistant variety that does well on less than ideal soils, and may be grown as a compact bush or large shrub. Introduced to commemorate the centenary of A E Housman's book of the same name.

Ballerina

A very pleasing and versatile rose with polyantha ancestry, and a forerunner of modern floribunda roses. The prolific tiny flowers appear in dense heads like a hydrangea, and are particularly good for cutting.

Season: Continuous summer and early autumn.

Foliage: Small mid-green, dense and glossy.

Height: Up to 1.5m (5ft)

Spread: Up to 1.8m (6ft)

Soil: Fertile, but tolerates poorer soils.

Positioning: Full sun or light shade; in borders and as ground cover, hedging, standards or in containers.

Care: No special care needed; manure well in autumn on lighter soils. Regular deadheading will help to maintain prolific flowering late in the season, sometimes until late autumn.

Pruning: Little necessary for shrubs. For lower ground cover prune lateral stems to downward-facing buds in spring.

Useful tips: May be pruned to fit a number of situations, to emphasize height or spread, for example. It also makes a dense hedge if planted 90cm (3ft) apart and clipped with shears in spring. 'Marjorie Fair' is a red version.

Bonica

Season: Repeat flowering early summer to early autumn.

Foliage: Small, glossy and deep green.

Height: 90cm–1.2m (3–4ft)

Spread: 1.2–1.5m (4–5ft)

Soil: Moist and fertile.

Positioning: Full sun; as ground cover or a spreading container plant. It can also be planted 60cm (2ft) apart to make an attractive rounded hedge.

Care: Benefits from generous mulching on drier soils; feed in spring and mid-summer.

Pruning: Growth is naturally prostrate, so the removal of dead and damaged wood in winter is the only attention necessary.

Useful tips: The spreading stems look very attractive arching from a large decorative container. The flower clusters are good for cutting. This variety is widely used by landscapers to cover large areas of ground, especially on banks that might be difficult to mow or plant with other species.

Sometimes known as 'Bonica 82', this very hardy modern shrub is one of the supreme ground cover cultivars and if well grown will spread tidily over a large area. The fully double flowers are borne in large sturdy clusters.

Bredon

Roses with this subtle colouring are rather special. Bredon's full and compact rosettes have a distinctive fruity fragrance and are produced with remarkable continuity on arching stems that emphasize the unusual elegance of the small bushes.

Season:	Repeat flowering all summer.
Foliage:	Large, shiny and dark green.
Height:	90cm (3ft)
Spread:	60cm (2ft)
Soil:	Fertile and well-cultivated, but tolerates poorer conditions.
Positioning:	Full sun, at the front of borders or in containers; ideal for smaller gardens. Restrained uniform growth and recurrent flowering make this a good choice for massing in small formal rose beds.
Care:	Very tough and survives well in a wide range of situations. Mulch in autumn and feed once or twice in summer for continuity of bloom.
Pruning:	Little needed; shorten leggy stems in winter to keep overall shape tidy.
Useful tips:	Try growing 2–3 plants in a medium-sized container, edged with trailing blue lobelia for contrast. May also be grown 45cm (18in) apart as a reliable low hedge.

Buff Beauty

Season:	Repeat flowering, mid-summer until autumn.
Foliage:	Dark green with purple tint, on strong arching stems.
Height:	1.2m (4ft) or more
Spread:	1.5m (5ft)
Soil:	All kinds, including light dry ground.
Positioning:	Full sun or dappled shade; as a specimen shrub or informal hedge.
Care:	Very drought-tolerant, but watering improves performance and health, and can also deter mildew. Mulch in spring.
Pruning:	Good formative pruning is important during the 2–3 seasons plants need to reach their full size. Careful shaping encourages upward growth. Deadhead faded trusses, cutting back to a strong side-shoot.
Useful tips:	Makes a fine hedge when planted 60cm (2ft) apart. Precautionary sprays against mildew will extend flowering season. An excellent variety for cutting.

Thought to be a seedling from the noisette 'William Allen Richardson', this is a lovely and vigorous hybrid musk with heavy trusses of tea-scented blooms, varying between apricot and creamy ivory according to age and exposure to sunlight.

Candy Rose

This bushy cluster-flowered modern shrub can be grown as a single specimen or in groups as robust ground cover for large gardens. The semi-double blooms are eye-catching, especially on a dull day, their rich colour compensating for small size and faint perfume.

Season:	Continuous all summer.
Foliage:	Medium green and glossy, on long lax stems.
Height:	1.2cm (4ft)
Spread:	1.8cm (6ft)
Soil:	Most well-drained kinds, including light soils.
Positioning:	Full sun or partial shade; in larger beds and borders, and as ground cover.
Care:	Plants are fairly drought-tolerant, but watering in dry weather encourages stronger growth and flowering. Mulch in spring and feed in late summer for enhanced performance.
Pruning:	Normally unnecessary; for lower ground cover shorten upper branches to downward-facing buds in late winter.
Useful tips:	Robust good health makes this an ideal choice for hot soils and disease-prone areas. Plant 90cm (3ft) apart to make a spreading hedge or edging to large beds, and as ground cover under deciduous trees.

Cardinal Hume

Season: Repeat flowering all summer.

Foliage: Matt, dark greyish-green.

Height: 1.2m (4ft)

Spread: 90cm (3ft)

Soil: Most kinds, including indifferent ground.

Positioning: Full sun or light shade; in borders or as bedding or hedges; also makes a spectacular display in a tub.

Care: No special care needed. Manure in autumn on poorer soils and mulch in spring. Deadhead after flowering.

Pruning: Robust growth requires little special pruning; shorten the length of strong stems in winter to tidy overall appearance and occasionally remove some older stems to induce new basal shoots.

Useful tips: Useful for cutting. Ideal for informal hedges when planted 45–60cm (18–24in) apart. For growing in tubs, choose a container about 45cm (18in) deep and 60cm (2ft) in diameter.

A dense spreading shrub with strong stems, valuable for its ability to thrive on lighter soils and for the rich sumptuous colour of its slightly fragrant blooms that deepens with age. A modern shrub rose with an old-fashioned appearance.

Charles Austin

This modern shrub makes a strong bush of vigorous upright growth, sometimes at the expense of its richly scented, very large blooms; harder than usual pruning is the secret of extending the flowering season through into autumn.

Season: Repeat flowering all summer (and sometimes autumn).

Foliage: Large and shapely mid-green leaves.

Height: 1.5m (5ft)

Spread: 1.2m (4ft)

Soil: Fairly rich and well-cultivated.

Positioning: Full sun; in larger borders or as a specimen shrub in mixed borders.

Care: Manure generously in autumn and mulch in spring on drier soils; feed at mid-summer to encourage later blooms.

Pruning: Prune lightly if a large bush is required. To ensure good continuity of bloom well into autumn, either prune hard in winter or early spring, or trim after the first flush.

Useful tips: 'Yellow Charles Austin' is a good lemon-yellow variant with the same habit and constitution. Both have a tendency eventually to become tall and ungainly; counteract this by occasionally hard pruning to less than half normal height.

Cornelia

Season: Repeat flowering summer and autumn.

Foliage: Dense and glossy, rich dark green.

Height: Up to 1.8m (6ft)

Spread: 1.5–2.1m (5–7ft)

Soil: Tolerates a wide range of soil conditions, although richer ground supports extended flowering.

Positioning: Full sun or light shade; in large beds and borders. Grow as a single hedge or, if you have plenty of space, as single specimens.

Care: Very adaptable and no special care needed. Manure lighter soils for best results, and mulch in spring.

Pruning: Trim lightly in winter. Withstands harder pruning if space is limited; remove up to one-half of stronger growth.

Useful tips: Excellent for cutting and as a dense informal hedge if planted 90cm–1.2m (3–4ft) apart; also effective grown against a high fence, pruned as a climber.

A strong but easygoing shrub for the larger garden, often at its best in autumn. It is extremely weather-resistant and rain seldom spoils the lavish display of highly fragrant flowers, invidually small but borne in large trusses.

Cottage Rose

A small and unassuming bush with glowing cupped blooms of really old-fashioned charm. Only lightly fragrant, but compensates by repeating remarkably well all summer on the numerous twiggy side-shoots. One of the best choices when space is limited.

Season: Repeats very well all summer.

Foliage: Mid-green, shiny and variable in shape on twiggy branching stems.

Height: 90cm–1.2m (3–4ft)

Spread: 75cm (2½ft)

Soil: Rich, moisture-retentive and deeply dug.

Positioning: Ideal for smaller gardens in full sun; as specimens or in small groups, as bedding or at the front of a border.

Care: Manure well in autumn, and mulch and feed in spring. Preventive sprays against mildew are advisable.

Pruning: Shorten the stronger stems by half in winter for large blooms and good repeat flowering, and remove dead wood, together some of the old stems as shrubs age.

Useful tips: Best kept as a small bush by firm pruning to ensure good blooms; needs very good growing conditions.

Cymbeline

Season: Repeat flowering in summer.

Foliage: Mid-green and serrated, fairly sparse on arching stems.

Height: 1.2m (4ft)

Spread: 1.5m (5ft)

Soil: Most soils if fertile and moisture-retentive.

Positioning: Full sun or light shade, with plenty of room to spread, in larger beds and borders. The pronounced arching growth makes an excellent contrast with more upright plants in a mixed border.

Care: Little special attention needed. Mulch well on drier soils.

Pruning: Remove dead and diseased wood in winter and trim lightly to shape in spring; may be pruned harder but looks best as a full-sized shrub.

Useful tips: Choose sites carefully as strongly coloured neighbours might easily diminish the gentle impact of the subtly coloured blooms. Try pegging down the lax stems to a surrounding rail to make a mound of blooms.

This modern shrub rose is fascinating for the unusually soft colouring of its large, loosely double blooms and its strong seductive scent. For all its restrained appearance, it is tough and hardy, with low maintenance requirements.

Dapple Dawn

Elegant and unobtrusive, with graceful stems bearing simple flowers that are delicately scented and saucer-shaped. Given shelter and good living conditions, this modern rose will prove very reliable, with a long summer sequence of bloom.

Season: Almost continuous throughout summer.

Foliage: Matt mid-green, small and curving, on slender stems.

Height: 1.5m (5ft)

Spread: 1.2m (4ft)

Soil: Rich and well-drained, with plenty of humus.

Positioning: Full sun and shelter from strong winds; in larger beds and borders.

Care: Often needs care with establishment: prepare the ground thoroughly, mulch and water as needed in the first season. Thereafter manure in autumn and mulch in spring.

Pruning: Shorten any long stems in early winter to avoid wind damage, and finally trim to shape in spring.

Useful tips: A sport of bright crimson 'Red Coat', which makes an ideal companion for this rose because of the close similarity in their flowering; however, 'Red Coat' tolerates harsher conditions and is generally more robust.

Eglantyne

Season: Repeat flowering all summer.

Foliage: Dark green, matt and well-formed on broad bushy stems.

Height: 90cm–1.2m (3–4ft)

Spread: 90–105cm (3–3½ft)

Soil: Most well-drained soils including less fertile kinds.

Positioning: Full sun or light shade; in beds and borders in groups or as a specimen.

Care: Undemanding. Mulch in spring with garden compost, and feed in spring and at mid-summer; manure in autumn on poorer soils.

Pruning: May be hard pruned in winter to maintain shape, or will make a larger shapely bush if lightly pruned.

Useful tips: Worth trying in a large container, positioned where the lovely perfume can be enjoyed. May suffer occasionally from mildew in some seasons: pruning to an open framework of branches and sprays of fungicide from mid-summer should prevent this.

A strong and spreading shrub with very attractive foliage and a neat bushy habit. The blooms are outstanding for their perfect shape and sweet scent. Small enough for a limited space, but adaptable and may be left to grow taller.

The vigorous and well-branched bushes will survive in a number of varied positions, and also in containers. A good flush of medium-sized flowers in large trusses appears in early summer and again in autumn after a distinct rest.

Season: Intermittent in summer and autumn.

Foliage: Small, glossy and mid-green on upright stems.

Height: 1.5–1.8m (5–6ft)

Spread: 1.2–1.5m (4–5ft)

Soil: Tolerates most soils including poor sites.

Positioning: Full sun or dappled shade; in larger beds and borders, and also on pillars.

Care: No special care needed. Mulch in spring, and feed after first flush of blooms on lighter soils.

Pruning: Remove dead and diseased wood in winter, and thin older stems where trained on pillars. May be pruned harder to keep bushes more compact.

Useful tips: Good for cut flowers, and also for strong hedges if planted 90cm (3ft) apart. The brilliant colour may be difficult to mix with other roses, so choose its neighbours carefully. Try growing in a half-barrel; surround the base of the rose with bold summer bedding.

English Garden

Season: Repeat flowering all summer.
Foliage: Large and rich green.
Height: 90cm (3ft)
Spread: 75cm (2½ft)
Soil: Rich, well-cultivated and free-draining.
Positioning: Full sun or light shade; near the front of borders and beds. An excellent variety for mass bedding because of its relatively short stature.
Care: Manure well in autumn and mulch in spring; feed in spring and again at mid-summer.
Pruning: Little special pruning needed, except to shorten excessively long stems in winter to keep shrubs neat and bushy.
Useful tips: A robust rose that makes a good container plant or formal group. Try combining this with another rose of similar habit, pink 'Charmian' for example, planting both in front of a summer-flowering honeysuckle or clematis.

A dependable and attractive rose, as might be expected with 'Iceberg' in its ancestry. The flowers are very large, with a complex old-fashioned appearance, and in good conditions are produced on compact bushes over a long season.

Escapade

Authorities disagree about the classification of this lovely variety, some regarding it as a shrub rose and others a floribunda. It succeeds as either, forming a vigorous leafy shrub with large striking blooms that have a pronounced scent of musk.

Season: Almost continuous all summer and into autumn.

Foliage: Light green, glossy and plentiful, on strong branching stems.

Height: 90cm (3ft)

Spread: 90cm (3ft)

Soil: Most free-draining and well-manured soils.

Positioning: Full sun or light shade; as a specimen bush or in small groups; also planted 45cm (18in) apart as a low hedge.

Care: Manure in autumn and mulch in spring, especially on lighter soils; feed in spring and mid-summer. Spray with systemic fungicide.

Pruning: May be pruned by removing dead and diseased wood in winter and then lightly trimming to shape. Alternatively cut out some old stems completely, shorten weaker shoots by half and lightly trim strong young stems.

Useful tips: A very good variety for cutting. Although once very healthy, disease resistance seems to be declining.

Season: Repeat flowering all summer.

Foliage: Rich green with a bronze tint on strong upright stems.

Height: 105cm (3½ft)

Spread: 90cm (3ft)

Soil: Fertile and well-drained.

Positioning: Full sun or light shade; in groups in prominent positions in beds and borders, or in containers.

Care: Manure in autumn and mulch in spring with garden compost; feed in spring and again at mid-summer. Support the heavy blooms in exposed positions.

Pruning: Remove dead and damaged wood in winter, together with some old stems from mature bushes, and prune lightly to shape.

Useful tips: With its upright growth and exceptional scent, this is a good variety for pot cultivation. It makes a fine cut flower, especially when combined with 'Golden Celebration' and the 'Alexandra Rose'.

Outstanding in many ways, especially for the high quality of its blooms which are densely folded and vary in colour from apricot or yellow through to pink depending on the time of year. Its fragrance is particularly captivating.

Fair Bianca

A sound healthy little rose, with densely folded blooms which are breathtaking in their snowy white perfection. They start life as neat rounded cups that open to full flattened saucers, the outer petals finally reflexing with age.

Season: Repeat flowering all summer.

Foliage: Dense, shapely and rich green in good soils, but may be sparse and paler elsewhere. The upright stems are covered in numerous small spines.

Height: 90cm (3ft)

Spread: 60cm (2ft)

Soil: Rich and well-drained, with plenty of humus.

Positioning: Full sun or light shade; in a conspicuous position near the front of beds and borders; also in informal groups and containers.

Care: Tolerates a wide range of conditions if manured well in autumn and mulched in spring; feed in spring.

Pruning: A naturally sturdy and upright rose, with no special pruning necessary: lightly trim to shape in winter.

Useful tips: A useful variety that stands out well in the garden. Light shade produces a creamy tinge at the base of the petals but enhances the strong myrrh fragrance.

Felicia

Season: Repeat flowering summer and autumn.

Foliage: Prolific, glossy and mid-green.

Height: 1.2–1.5m (4–5ft)

Spread: 1.5–1.8m (5–6ft)

Soil: Moist and fertile, but tolerates a wide range.

Positioning: Full sun or semi-shade; in larger beds and borders; also as a hedge and in containers.

Care: Manure in autumn, and on light soils mulch well in spring; feed at mid-summer to sustain the good autumn display.

Pruning: No special requirements: either prune lightly for large bushes, or cut back to half in winter for a more compact shape.

Useful tips: As the best displays often occur in autumn, site this where it gets maximum sunlight late in the year. For really dramatic impact, allow a clematis such as mauve-pink 'Twilight' to scramble through the rose branches and blend with the late summer flowers.

A lovely and enduring old rose, one of the finest hybrid musks. Bushes are upright and spread luxuriantly from a well-branched base, the strong stems bearing heavy clusters of silvery pink flowers, deeper in the centres and fully 7cm (3in) across.

Fiona

With its exceptionally strong growth, this is one of the largest ground cover roses, also useful as a bush given careful pruning. The rich blood-red flowers are small but dramatic, their free appearance all season making up for lack of size.

Season:	Repeat flowering summer and early autumn.
Foliage:	Dense, small and glossy rich green.
Height:	75cm (30in)
Spread:	1.2–1.8m (4–6ft)
Soil:	Fertile and well-drained.
Positioning:	Full sun; for massed planting and ground cover in larger beds and borders, or as a spreading specimen near the front. Excellent for covering steep banks or trailing over a low wall.
Care:	Mulch well on light soils; manure in autumn or feed in spring and again at mid-summer.
Pruning:	Cut out dead wood in winter and trim to limit spread in spring; shorten any strong upright shoots.
Useful tips:	To produce a hedge plant against wire netting, 45cm (18in) apart and train the spreading stems in an upright fan. Will also make an imaginative choice for growing in a wide container, allowing the branches to arch over the sides.

Season: Early summer to early winter.

Foliage: Mid- to dark green, tough and shiny.

Height: 60cm (2ft)

Spread: 90cm–1.2m (3–4ft)

Soil: Fairly rich and well-cultivated, with plenty of humus.

Positioning: Full sun; as ground cover and edging for larger borders, on banks and in containers, and also grafted as standards.

Care: Enjoys lavish conditions, so manure well in autumn and mulch in spring with garden compost, and feed in spring and mid-summer.

Pruning: Minimal. Remove dead and diseased wood in winter and lightly trim to shape.

Useful tips: With its fine colour and continuity of bloom, makes a stunning weeping standard, especially in a decorative container. Provides a solid support for a freely trailing clematis such as *orientalis* 'Helios'.

Noted for its tough and healthy constitution and long flowering season, especially in a warm summer. If fed lavishly this attractive ground cover variety has an enormous crop of blooms, with a distinctly old-fashioned appearance.

A large attractive shrub, whose outstanding blooms are almost classic hybrid tea in shape and appear both singly and in small trusses. With care may be pruned as a pillar rose or even a medium-sized climber.

Season: Repeat flowering all summer.

Foliage: Large, shiny and dark green, reddish when young.

Height: 1.8m (6ft)

Spread: 90cm–1.2m (3–4ft)

Soil: Rich and well-cultivated.

Positioning: Full sun; as a specimen bush or pillar rose, in containers or as a tall hedge (but not exposed to strong autumn winds).

Care: Manure well in autumn, and feed at mid-summer. Deadhead after flowering.

Pruning: Remove all dead and diseased wood in winter, and some of the older stems to encourage new basal growth. In spring tidy any tall shoots damaged by wind.

Useful tips: This makes an excellent hedge when planted 45cm (18in) apart. As a precaution against injury, taller stems may be shortened in autumn, leaving the rest of the pruning until the end of the winter.

Season: Early summer and intermittently later.
Foliage: Mid-green, glossy and plentiful.
Height: 1.5–1.8m (5–6ft)
Spread: 1.2–1.5m (4–5ft)
Soil: Most kinds are suitable if moist and fertile.
Positioning: Full sun or light shade; as specimens or groups at the back of larger rose borders; also in mixed borders, containers and as a hedge.
Care: Manure in autumn and mulch in spring, especially on lighter soils. Deadhead and feed after the first main flush of blooms.
Pruning: Trim lightly to shape in winter to maintain full size, or cut back strong stems by one-third to one-half for more compact bushes.
Useful tips: A large vigorous bush worth trying as a specimen in grass. Although primarily a border rose, may be pruned harder for massing in large beds with other hybrid musks.

One of Reverend J Pemberton's fine hybrid musks, the handsome large sprays of loose single or semi-double apricot flowers have a strong aromatic fragrance. They are borne on very strong branches, dark red and arching gracefully.

Francine Austin

Although recommended as ground cover for larger areas, this shrub has arching rather than prostrate growth, its dainty sprays of shining white pompons appearing on slender wiry stems, well spaced out on sturdy plants.

Season: Repeat flowering all summer.

Foliage: Pale green leaflets, long and narrow.

Height: 90–105cm (3–3½ft)

Spread: 1.2m (4ft)

Soil: Most fertile, well-drained soils are suitable.

Positioning: Full sun or light shade; in larger borders as groups of shrubs or for ground cover, or in smaller gardens as specimen bushes.

Care: Mulch in spring, and feed in spring and mid-summer.

Pruning: As ground cover, prune to a downward-facing bud in winter to shape growth; hard pruning, removing half the new growth, will produce small bushy plants with plenty of new growth at the base. Alternatively prune lightly to build up full arching growth.

Useful tips: A single plant is very attractive trained as a small climber on a warm wall.

Fred Loads

Season: Repeat flowering all summer.

Foliage: Prolific, glossy and light green.

Height: 1.8m (6ft)

Spread: 90cm–1.2m (3–4ft)

Soil: Rich and well-drained.

Positioning: Full sun; as specimen shrubs in large beds and borders, or as a flowering hedge.

Care: Undemanding. Mulch lavishly in spring on light soils, water in dry weather and feed at mid-summer.

Pruning: Keep a sequence of stems of varying length by removing some older growth annually from the base and only lightly pruning younger stems.

Useful tips: For an effective bright hedge, plant 60cm (2ft) apart. Match carefully with other strongly coloured shrubs nearby. Useful as a cut flower, on its own or arranged with cut blue or mauve clematis; may also be grown with a clematis such as *texensis* 'Princess of Wales'.

For a brilliant splash of colour this variety is supreme when in full flower. Individually the flowers are very simple and almost single, but they are gathered in enormous trusses that can reach 45cm (18in) across to make a memorable impact.

Glamis Castle

One of the best whites, with a good strong scent of myrrh. The flowers are very old-fashioned in appearance, and look pretty and buoyant *en masse*, with the freedom and habit of a floribunda. With its low bushy growth, it deserves space in any garden.

Season: Good continuity throughout summer.

Foliage: Bright green and elegant, on light twiggy stems.

Height: 90cm (3ft)

Spread: 75–90cm (2½–3ft)

Soil: Rich and well-cultivated, with plenty of humus.

Positioning: Full sun; in groups as a bedding rose or at the front of borders, and as specimen bushes in small gardens and containers.

Care: Rich living produces the best results, so manure heavily in autumn, mulch in spring, and feed in spring and at mid-summer.

Pruning: Prune fairly lightly, in the same way as a floribunda.

Useful tips: As a short free-growing variety, worth trying as a flowering hedge, planting bushes 45cm (18in) apart and also for massing at the same distances in a bed to itself.

Golden Wings

Season: Continuous throughout summer.

Foliage: Glossy, light green and slightly pointed.

Height: 1.5–1.8m (5–6ft)

Spread: 1.2–1.5m (4–5ft)

Soil: Most are suitable, including light and impoverished ground.

Positioning: Full sun or light shade; as a free-standing bush or an attractive hedge.

Care: Mulch freely on light soils, and manure in autumn. Remove old faded blooms to ensure good continuity.

Pruning: Cut out a few old branches annually to encourage new growth, and shorten tall stems by one-third in winter. Prune hedges firmly for good density.

Useful tips: An ideal choice for difficult soils, or where blooms might be damaged by wind and rain. Plant 60cm (2ft) apart for hedging, for which this variety is especially suitable. It also combines well with a rich blue clematis such as 'Rhapsody'.

Universally praised as perhaps the best large-flowered yellow shrub, this is a strong bushy plant with relatively few thorns. Although free-flowering, quality is the main characteristic of the large single blooms with their clear colour and refreshing scent.

An excellent shrub, notable for its vigorous, slightly arching bushy growth, and for its glowing yellow tea-scented flowers with the form of old-fashioned peonies and a warmth of colour unique among modern roses.

Season:	Repeat flowering early summer to late autumn.
Foliage:	Shiny, mid-green.
Height:	1.2m (4ft)
Spread:	1.2m (4ft)
Soil:	Fairly rich and well-cultivated.
Positioning:	Full sun; as specimens in beds and borders, and also in containers.
Care:	Manure well in autumn, mulch in spring, and feed in spring and at mid-summer.
Pruning:	Trim lightly to shape in early spring, and remove one or two older stems annually when bushes are established. In a warm season, may produce some very tall shoots which should be cut well back to maintain a rounded outline.
Useful tips:	Flowers are good for cutting, and this (or occasional deadheading) will help to extend the flowering season. If pruned lightly may be trained as a short climber against a wall or pillar.

Season: Repeat flowering in summer.

Foliage: Mid-green, glossy and prolific.

Height: 45cm (18in)

Spread: 2.1m (7ft)

Soil: Any well-drained soil, including those of poorer quality.

Positioning: Full sun; as ground cover and for trailing from walls or down banks; also grafted as weeping standards.

Care: Undemanding if ground prepared thoroughly before planting. Mulch with garden compost in spring; feed in spring and again at mid-summer.

Pruning: Remove dead or injured branches in winter, and trim lightly to shape.

Useful tips: One of several varieties with the names of game birds, such as 'Pheasant' and 'Partridge', all of which combine well as mixed ground cover.

Highly effective at covering large areas of ground and suppressing weeds with its abundant foliage, this is a naturally very prostrate variety that will mould itself to contours and trail or climb over undulating ground.

Heather Austin

Very modern and yet typically old-fashioned in appearance, colour and fragrance. The blooms are attractive at all stages, and form lovely flattened balls before opening fully into deep, very large open cups.

Season:	Repeat flowering all summer.
Foliage:	Neat and bright green, the leaflets spaced well apart.
Height:	90cm–1.8m (3–6ft)
Spread:	75cm (2½ft)
Soil:	Any fertile and well-drained ground.
Positioning:	Full sun or light shade; in groups in larger borders or as specimen plants, and also as a short climber on walls and pillars. Try planting a group of three, spaced 60cm (2ft) apart, as a central feature in a round formal bed.
Care:	Manure in autumn, and mulch and feed in spring.
Pruning:	Cut back young growth by half for bushy shrubs and large blooms, or prune lightly for taller bushes; also train as a climber by thinning and tying in the strongest stems.
Useful tips:	Plants are very tough and adaptable. Try fanning out as a climber on a slightly shaded wall.

Heavenly Rosalind

Season: Intermittently all summer.

Foliage: Small and greyish-green, like an Alba rose.

Height: 1.2–1.5m (4–5ft)

Spread: 1.2m (4ft)

Soil: Fertile and well-drained, with plenty of humus.

Positioning: Full sun or light shade; in groups or as a specimen shrub, at the back of rose borders or in mixed borders.

Care: Manure well in autumn, mulch in spring, and feed spring and mid-summer.

Pruning: Prune lightly, especially at first, to build up a strong shapely shrub, and then remove dead wood in winter together with one or two old branches where they can be spared.

Useful tips: A good-looking shrub that would deserve prominence almost anywhere in the garden, especially among other kinds of shrubs.

A fairly new introduction with all the appearance of an old species or wild rose. It is very tough and disease-resistant, and has sufficient vigour to maintain a good continuity of bloom all season. The attractive foliage enhances the overall effect.

Although a modern rose, this has the classic perfection of old-fashioned varieties, its blooms packed with densely folded petals restrained by neatly cupped outer rows. The colour is delicate and consistent and the fragrance surprisingly strong.

Season: Repeat flowering all summer.

Foliage: Large and dark green, on strong stems that are slightly arching at first.

Height: 1.2m (4ft)

Spread: 1.2m (4ft)

Soil: Rich and well-drained, although fairly tolerant of most soils if fertility is kept high.

Positioning: Full sun; as specimens or prominent groups in beds and borders, and also in containers.

Care: Prefers lavish conditions, so manure ground well before planting and then top-dress annually in autumn; feed at mid-summer for continuity.

Pruning: Early lax growth can be shortened to upward-facing buds; otherwise no special requirements.

Useful tips: The lingering lemon fragrance is addictive, so site bushes where this can be appreciated.

Hilda Murrell

Season:	Early summer; light crop late summer.
Foliage:	Dark green with serrated edges, on stout vigorous stems that are very thorny.
Height:	1.2m (4ft)
Spread:	1.2m (4ft)
Soil:	Fertile and well-cultivated, but succeeds on a wide range of sites.
Positioning:	Full sun; in beds and borders.
Care:	For best results enrich the ground well before planting and mulch annually with well-rotted manure; a mid-summer feed improves later flowering. Deadhead after the first flush of blooms.
Pruning:	No special pruning needed; trim lightly to shape in winter.
Useful tips:	Site this where you can enjoy the perfume and early summer display, but where other roses or shrubs take over later in the season, as secondary flowering in late summer is only a certainty in very warm and sheltered gardens.

Although the limited flowering season resembles that of older roses, this modern shrub is worth growing for its robust indifference to harsh conditions and for the shining intensity of its large flowers with their rosettes of thickly folded petals.

Thanks to its partly Scottish rose ancestry, this is a bushy and vigorous variety that looks superb grown against a dark fence or wall. The blooms are large, 10cm (4in) across, and daintily scalloped around the edges, with a light musk fragrance.

Season: Repeat flowering all summer and autumn, in repeat flushes up to the first frosts.

Foliage: Dark green and glossy.

Height: 1.5–1.8m (5–6ft)

Spread: 1.5–1.8m (5–6ft)

Soil: Rich, well-cultivated and free-draining.

Positioning: Full sun; in larger beds and borders, against walls and fences, and as a hedge.

Care: Manure in autumn and mulch well in spring, especially on lighter soils; watering in dry weather is essential.

Pruning: Shaping the bushes after flowering is the only essential. Prune hedges more firmly to encourage high density.

Useful tips: Plant 90cm (3ft) apart for a strong, bushy and very attractive flowering hedge. The length of flowering season is an outstanding quality of this rose, making it suitable for many purposes, even for large-scale massed bedding.

Jacquenetta

Season: Early summer with good repeats, especially in autumn.

Foliage: Mid-green, strong and attractive.

Height: 1.5–1.8m (5–6ft)

Spread: 1.2m (4ft)

Soil: Most soils are suitable, including poorer kinds.

Positioning: Full sun or light to semi-shade; as a specimen shrub towards the back of larger borders.

Care: Undemanding. Manure in autumn, and feed in spring; mulch lighter soils well in spring, and feed in spring and at mid-summer.

Pruning: Light pruning, just tipping shoots and reducing strong stems by up to one-third in winter, will retain the large contours, but bushes may also be pruned hard where space is limited.

Useful tips: If planted against a wall or fence, this variety may be trained as a short climber, adding 60cm (2ft) or so to its height; try growing with the herbaceous Clematis × durandii for an exciting partnership.

A popular modern shrub rose, its attractive semi-double apricot flowers always draw praise. It is a tough variety, coping with far from perfect sites, and makes an unusually large vigorous bush, ideal for providing height in the border.

John Clare

The lovely and informal, strong pink or light crimson cup-shaped blooms are less than perfect in shape, but this is more than outweighed by the exuberant quantity of blooms. It is one of the best varieties for late flowers.

Season: Repeat flowering all season, especially in autumn.

Foliage: Bright green and large, on fairly thornless stems.

Height: 90cm–1.2m (3–4ft)

Spread: 75–90cm (2½–3ft)

Soil: Rich and well-cultivated, with plenty of humus to help retain moisture.

Positioning: Full sun or light shade; singly or in groups near the front of rose and mixed borders.

Care: Prepare the ground thoroughly before planting, working in generous amouts of well-rotted manure to raise fertility levels. Manure in autumn and mulch in spring; feed in spring and at mid-summer.

Pruning: May be pruned lightly for larger shrubs, but will not repeat as well as shorter bushes pruned hard in late winter to half their height.

Useful tips: Worth trying as a hedge, planted 45cm (18in) apart and trimmed every year to about 60cm (2ft).

Season: Good continuity all summer.

Foliage: Bright green and shapely, on arching stems.

Height: 105cm (3½ft)

Spread: 1.2m (4ft)

Soil: Rich and well-drained.

Positioning: Full sun; as full-size bushes in large borders, as specimens or in groups, or pruned more severely for smaller rose and mixed borders.

Care: Manure in autumn, mulch and feed in spring. May need spraying against rust: in a close humid season or a very dry summer when plants may be under stress, precautionary sprays of fungicide every 2–3 weeks should prevent problems occurring.

Pruning: Either prune lightly in winter to encourage spreading growth, or cut back by one-third to one-half to keep bushes more compact.

Useful tips: Try growing in a sheltered position to shield blooms from rain and accentuate their scent.

The outstanding fragrance, for which this variety has won international prizes, compensates for the tendency of blooms not to open fully in wet weather. Bushes are free-flowering, however, and this is only an occasional fault.

La Sevillana

A modern rose with a complex ancestry that includes the renowned 'Super Star', which explains the intensity of its colour. Plants are very hardy and easygoing as long as they are in full sun, and flower profusely with heavy trusses of blooms.

Season:	Continuous all summer.
Foliage:	Glossy and rich green with bronze tints.
Height:	1.2m (4ft)
Spread:	1.2m (4ft)
Soil:	Tolerates most kinds if fertile and well-drained.
Positioning:	Full sun and an open position are essential; as a specimen in beds and borders, or as a hedge. In some soils makes more lateral growth than height, and could be useful for ground cover.
Care:	Manure in autumn and mulch in spring. Deadheading improves later flowering.
Pruning:	Shorten younger stems by about one-third in winter and remove one or two older stems to encourage new growth. For ground cover shorten more upright stems and prune arching growth back to downward facing buds.
Useful tips:	Plant 45–60cm (18–24in) apart for a bold and reliable hedge, and trim to shape in late winter.

L D Braithwaite

Season: Repeat flowering all summer.

Foliage: Large, dark green or greyish-green and glossy on spreading stems.

Height: 105cm (3½ft)

Spread: 105cm (3½ft)

Soil: Rich and well-cultivated.

Positioning: Full sun or light shade; as specimens or groups in rose or mixed borders.

Care: Responds to good growing conditions, so manure in autumn and mulch in spring; also feed in spring and at mid-summer.

Pruning: Cut back young growth firmly in winter by one-third; or prune more lightly to encourage the naturally broad open shape or for a larger than normal shrub.

Useful tips: An extravert rose that deserves an eye-catching position. With its relatively low growth and remarkable continuity of flowering, this variety can be used for effective massed bedding.

Unlike many red varieties, this one has an excellent health status and is also slow to fade. Its brilliant crimson blooms stand out well and demand attention, as much for their wide full-petalled form as for their opulent colour.

Leander

Vigorous open growth with long slender stems that can reach 4m (13ft) long, making this an ideal climber as well as specimen bush. The strongly fruit-scented blooms are small, but borne in lavish open trusses and perfectly formed.

Season: Early summer and occasional second flowering.

Foliage: Mid- to dark green and shiny.

Height: 1.8m (6ft)

Spread: 1.5m (5ft)

Soil: Most kinds if fertile and well-cultivated.

Positioning: Full sun or light shade; as a specimen in large beds and borders, or trained as a climber.

Care: Robust and hardy, little special care needed. Mulch in spring, and deadhead and feed after the first flush of bloom.

Pruning: As a shrub, remove dead wood in winter and one or two older stems, and prune lightly; as a climber minimal pruning except for the removal of dead and exhausted wood.

Useful tips: Train as a climber by tying in a few of the stronger stems against a wall or trellis, and combine with a late-flowering clematis.

Lucetta

Season: Mid-summer.

Foliage: Prolific and dark green, with a highly polished finish, on strong arching stems.

Height: 1.2m (4ft)

Spread: 1.2m (4ft)

Soil: Rich and well-drained, but tolerates less than ideal sites.

Positioning: Full sun with shelter from strong winds; as a specimen in beds and borders, or as a climber.

Care: Manure in autumn and mulch in spring. The arching stems may need support on lighter soils when fully laden.

Pruning: Remove dead wood in winter, plus one or two older stems to encourage regrowth; also shorten tall whippy stems by half.

Useful tips: May be trained as a climber, on a pillar or against a wall, when it will reach 3m (10ft) high. Group three together to produce the impression of a substantial shrub as a single specimen may look too open and sparse.

A very beautiful and satisfying rose, vigorous and extremely healthy, bearing enormous flowers that start as pretty buds, singly or in small clusters, and extend to 15cm (6in) across when fully open.

Many Happy Returns

Season: Continuously summer and autumn.

Foliage: Prolific, dark and shiny, on vigorous spreading branches.

Height: 90cm (3ft)

Spread: 90cm–1.2m (3–4ft)

Soil: Most fertile soils are suitable.

Positioning: Full sun; as a specimen or for mass planting in beds and borders, also in containers.

Care: Very hardy and resilient, with no special needs; a mid-summer feed helps sustain the long season. Deadhead after flowering, but if the late autumn crop of attractive hips is required, leave the last faded trusses of flowers untrimmed.

Pruning: Prune in winter, removing dead and diseased wood; shorten strong stems by one-third and leave thinner ones untouched.

Useful tips: One of the best varieties for growing in a container or in groups as highlights in a mixed border.

Sometimes classed as a floribunda, this is a modern shrub rose with a remarkably long flowering season, starting early in summer and often lasting until late autumn. The flowers are neat and produced in great quantities, enhancing almost any situation.

Season: Early summer and early autumn.

Foliage: Small, matt and pale green on long dark stems.

Height: 2.1–2.4m (7–8ft)

Spread: 2.1m (7ft)

Soil: Most kinds suitable; tolerates poor soil.

Positioning: Full sun; as a specimen in large beds and borders, in woodland surroundings, and also trained on a wall.

Care: Little needed. Mulch annually on lighter soils. The main flush of blooms occurs in early summer, but supplementary feeding in spring and again in early summer will help encourage later flowers.

Pruning: Remove dead and spindly growth in winter, and shorten very strong stems by one-third. Trim hedges to shape in winter.

Useful tips: Plant 1.2m (4ft) apart for hedging. Watch out for black spot disease, and spray with a systemic fungicide. Do not deadhead as the hips are attractive in autumn.

Often referred to as a pink 'Nevada' and sometimes as a form of Rosa moyesii, this very vigorous and dense shrub has the overall appearance of a wild rose, although the stems are not very thorny and the large blooms often repeat intermittently.

Exceptional disease resistance is one widely praised quality; another is the free branching habit that ensures a constant supply of new flowering side-shoots, so that the sweetly scented blooms continue to appear over a particularly long season.

Season: Repeat flowering summer and autumn.

Foliage: Matt, mid-green and plentiful.

Height: 1.2m (4ft)

Spread: 1.2m (4ft)

Soil: Most fertile soils are suitable.

Positioning: Full sun or light shade; in beds and borders or in containers; a group of three soon makes a striking feature, especially as this helps create a more substantial shrub, hiding the rather uneven growth.

Care: No special care needed. Mulch in spring, and feed in spring and at mid-summer.

Pruning: Thin some of the twiggy growth in winter, plus one or two old stems from mature bushes, and shorten any vigorous stems by one-third.

Useful tips: A very adaptable rose, worth considering for less than ideal positions. With their good length of stem, cut blooms are ideal for flower arrangements.

Mistress Quickly

Season: Repeats well all summer.

Foliage: Dark grey-green and small, like a noisette rose.

Height: 1.2m (4ft)

Spread: 90cm (3ft)

Soil: Most well-drained soils, including less fertile ones.

Positioning: Full sun or light shade; as specimens or small groups, behind other roses or in a prominent position in rose and mixed borders.

Care: Mulch in spring, especially on poorer soils where an autumn dressing of manure is also beneficial; feed in spring.

Pruning: Prune hard in winter for smaller well-flowering bushes or lightly for larger shrubs.

Useful tips: Strong growing as a climber, up to 1.8m (6ft) high, against a wall or trellis – train in stronger stems as a permanent framework and shorten side-shoots after flowering.

Robust, reliable and totally disease-resistant, this sound garden variety for any situation is a descendant of 'Blush Noisette' and shares the latter's dainty attractive foliage and small flower size. A lovely rose trained on an old brick wall.

Moonbeam

Confining choice to tough resilient varieties would mean missing a treasure like this, with its slender stems that bear simple but immaculate blooms, star-like in their symmetry, with perfectly sculpted petals.

Season:	Repeat flowering summer and autumn.
Foliage:	Dark green and delicate.
Height:	1.2m (4ft)
Spread:	1.2m (4ft)
Soil:	Rich and well-drained, with plenty of humus.
Positioning:	Full sun with protection from strong winds; in sheltered beds and borders, or in containers.
Care:	Needs good maintenance, so prepare the ground well before planting, manure in autumn and mulch in spring; a mid-summer feed is also beneficial.
Pruning:	Remove dead and diseased wood in winter, and shorten any wind-damaged stems in spring, before lightly pruning to shape.
Useful tips:	An especially attractive rose for ornamental containers in a sheltered spot, such as a sunny patio.

Moonlight

Season: Continuously summer and autumn.

Foliage: Dark with reddish tints, on mahogany stems.

Height: 1.5–1.8m (5–6ft)

Spread: 1.2–1.5m (4–5ft)

Soil: Most fertile free-draining soils are suitable.

Positioning: Full sun or light shade; as a specimen in large beds and borders, trained on a pillar or grown as a hedge. Virtually weather-proof and therefore worth considering for an exposed position.

Care: Manure in autumn, mulch in spring and water in dry weather; on poorer soils feed in spring and again at mid-summer. Watch out for mildew and spray with a systemic fungicide if necessary.

Pruning: Trim to shape in spring, reducing the overall size by one-third. May also be pruned more firmly to restrict size.

Useful tips: Plant 90cm (3ft) apart for hedging. Plants bear reddish-orange hips in autumn.

An old and richly scented hybrid musk that can tolerate wide extremes of soil and weather. The creamy white blooms are lemon yellow in bud and borne in very large clusters which contrast perfectly with the dark foliage and stems.

Morning Mist

A single rose of exceptional beauty, with some resemblance to old-fashioned Alba varieties, hence its suggestion of a species rose. Bushes are well-branched but airy, bearing bright red shapely buds in great profusion.

Season:	Continuous all summer.
Foliage:	Large, bright green and serrated.
Height:	1.5m (5ft)
Spread:	1.2m (4ft)
Soil:	Most fertile soils, including lighter kinds.
Positioning:	Full sun; as groups or single specimens in beds and borders; also succeeds planted singly or in groups in grass.
Care:	Manure poorer soils well in autumn and mulch in spring; feed in spring and at mid-summer.
Pruning:	Shorten strong growth by half after flowering and remove one or two old stems to encourage fresh young growth from the base.
Useful tips:	Worth trying in a container for its unusual habit and colour, or against a wall, where its open graceful stems can be fanned out or trained to produce a short climber. A variety worth experimenting with: try combining with a restrained blue clematis such as 'Lady Northcliffe'.

Mountbatten

Season: Continuous all summer.

Foliage: Crisp, rich green and leathery.

Height: 1.5m (5ft)

Spread: 1.2m (4ft)

Soil: Most fertile kinds, and tolerates poorer ground.

Positioning: Full sun; as massed bedding or single specimens in beds and borders; also as a container plant.

Care: Manure in autumn and mulch in spring. Deadhead after flowering and feed at mid-summer.

Pruning: Remove dead and diseased wood in winter, together with one or two old stems, and shorten all strong stems by one-third to one-half.

Useful tips: Planted 45–60cm (18–24in) apart this makes an excellent upright hedge that may be pruned lightly or more firmly depending on the desired height. Although borne in clusters, individual blooms often have sufficiently long stems to make their cutting for vases worthwhile.

Sometimes classed as a floribunda, but more like a very dense modern shrub in habit, bushy and highly disease-resistant. It is happy almost anywhere in the garden, given a sunny position where its leaves will prove almost evergreen.

A large shrub, thought to be related to *Rosa moyesii*, with dense arching growth that is sadly prone to black spot. One of the most popular shrubs, noted for its large flowers, 10cm (4in) across, that cover bushes during the first early summer flush.

Season: Early summer, followed by smaller intermittent flushes.

Foliage: Small, dark green and glossy.

Height: 2.4m (8ft)

Spread: 2.1m (7ft)

Soil: Most kinds, including light infertile soils.

Positioning: Full sun or light shade; as a specimen in larger borders, or trained against a wall. Space is important: very hard pruning to limit size is usually disappointing and plants need to spread to their full dimensions.

Care: Manure in autumn and mulch in spring on lighter soils. Deadhead and feed after the first main flush of blooms.

Pruning: Cut out up to one-third of old stems annually to encourage vigorous young growth, and shorten strong side-shoots by one-third.

Useful tips: May be troubled by black spot and need spraying with a systemic fungicide. Try growing on a pillar between *Clematis montana* varieties.

Noble Antony

Season: Repeats well all summer.

Foliage: Large and dark green, on short upright stems.

Height: 90cm (3ft)

Spread: 75–90cm (2½–3ft)

Soil: Fertile and well-drained.

Positioning: Full sun, with plenty of space; as specimens or in small groups at the front of rose and mixed borders. Planted in groups of two, three or more, individual plants merge to form a dense substantial shrub with greater continuity of blooms.

Care: Manure in autumn and mulch in spring; feed in spring and at mid-summer.

Pruning: Shorten young growth by half in winter (firm pruning encourages good blooms), or lightly trim for larger plants.

Useful tips: With its small bushy growth, an excellent variety for containers and also for semi-formal bedding. May also be grown as an eye-catching dwarf hedge, about 45cm (18in) apart.

An excellent dark, almost brooding rose with deep crimson blooms of immaculate form, full of petals that turn back at the edges to form a perfect dome. Give it a prominent position, free from competition, to emphasize its good qualities.

Nozomi

An outstanding Japanese variety, strictly a climbing or trailing miniature but widely used for lavish ground cover plantings and for edging large beds. The slender stems are covered with great quantities of the small flowers, white or pearly pink.

Season: Continuous during summer.
Foliage: Small, dark green and glossy.
Height: 60cm (2ft)
Spread: 1.8–2.4m (6–8ft)
Soil: Most fertile soils are suitable.
Positioning: Full sun; as ground cover in larger beds and borders, as a trailer or climber trained on a fence, and grafted as a standard.
Care: Where the dense growth permits, mulch in spring on lighter soils or feed in spring and at mid-summer. Peg down the arching stems for good ground coverage.
Pruning: Very little needed. Remove one or two old stems to make way for new growth.
Useful tips: Outstanding as a cascading rose, trailing from the top of a wall or bank, or as a weeping standard. With its small flowers and leaves, also looks appropriate planted in a large rock garden.

Nur Mahal

Season: Early summer and intermittently until autumn.

Foliage: Large, dark and glossy.

Height: 1.5m (5ft)

Spread: 1.2m (4ft)

Soil: Most kinds including impoverished soil.

Positioning: Full sun or light shade; as a specimen bush or colourful hedge. Like all hybrid musks, makes a good shrub for mixed borders, or may be pruned more heavily and massed in a large bed.

Care: No special care required on rich soils; elsewhere manure in autumn and mulch in spring. Feed in early spring and again after the first main flush of blooms.

Pruning: Shorten strong stems by one-third in winter, and remove one or two old branches to encourage new wood.

Useful tips: Plant 60cm (2ft) apart for a robust hedge likely to succeed in unfavourable positions.

One of the many fine hybrid musks bred by Reverend Pemberton, although not as common as it should be these days. An easygoing shrub for many sites, with graceful growth and a profusion of neat dusky flowers in large clusters in early summer, followed by orange hips.

Nymphenburg

A dense upright shrub, with strong arching stems well clad with broad, richly coloured leaves. The flowers have a sweet apple scent and can reach 10cm (4in) across, making this a spectacular climbing or hedging variety.

Season: Repeat flowering all summer.

Foliage: Lush, dark green and glossy.

Height: 1.8m (6ft)

Spread: 1.5m (5ft)

Soil: Any fertile kind; tolerates poorer soils.

Positioning: Full sun; variously as specimens, hedging and climbing roses, and also in containers.

Care: No special care needed, but autumn manuring and a spring mulch advisable in poorer soils.

Pruning: Shorten vigorous new stems of bushes by one-third in winter and remove one or two old branches to encourage renewal.

Useful tips: Trained as a climber or pillar rose, this may reach 3.6m (12ft) or more in height and also cover a greater spread than as a shrub – fan the arching stems out to produce an even framework of branches. The colour may vary considerably according to soil or weather conditions.

Season: Repeat flowering all season.

Foliage: Small and dark green, with well-spaced leaflets.

Height: 1.2m (4ft)

Spread: 90cm (3ft)

Soil: Fertile and well-drained.

Positioning: Full sun; as specimens or groups, in rose or mixed borders. With their short twiggy growth, bushes are ideal for a front-of-border position.

Care: Manure in autumn and mulch in spring; feed spring and mid-summer on poorer soils. Deadhead after first flush to ensure continuity of bloom. Spray occasionally with fungicide.

Pruning: Prune younger stems back by half in winter and trim others lightly to maintain neat upright habit.

Useful tips: Choose whether to deadhead after the first main flush, which will encourage later blooms, or leave faded flowers for an autumn display of hips.

Not the best for disease resistance, but still a lovely rose, especially when seen *en masse* covered with a froth of the dainty pale blush-coloured blooms. Especially effective with the light behind the delicate, almost transparent petals.

Penelope

One of the best hybrid musks, handsome and reliable, with dense spreading growth very tolerant of poor conditions. The large clusters of blooms are prolific in early summer and even more so in autumn. An essential rose for any shrub collection.

Season: Continuously summer and autumn.

Foliage: Large, fairly glossy and bronze tinted.

Height: 1.5–1.8m (5–6ft)

Spread: 1.2–1.5m (4–5ft)

Soil: Best in fertile ground but tolerates most kinds.

Positioning: Full sun or light shade; in beds and borders of all sizes, as a specimen and as a hedge.

Care: Manure poor soils in autumn and mulch in spring. Deadhead during summer, and feed once or twice to sustain the display.

Pruning: Remove some of the old stems in winter and shorten vigorous young shoots. Can be pruned harder to maintain a height of 90cm (3ft).

Useful tips: In good ground will make a highly ornamental hedge, but do not deadhead if you want the coral pink hips in autumn. Watch out for mildew in hot summers.

Pink Bells

Season: Repeat flowering in summer.

Foliage: Small, glossy and dark green, in masses.

Height: 75cm (2½ft)

Spread: 1.2–1.5m (4–5ft)

Soil: Most kinds if fertile and well-drained.

Positioning: Full sun; as ground cover in beds and borders, and also trained on a low fence.

Care: Mulch in spring or feed at mid-summer, and manure poorer soils in autumn. Deadhead after flowering.

Pruning: Little needed, apart from trimming in winter to maintain a neat shape; shorten any tall vertical shoots to maintain low profile.

Useful tips: An ideal rose for fanning against a wire-netting fence to produce a flowering hedge. 'Red Bells' and 'White Bells' are close relatives and good companions. In some seasons flowering is limited to just four weeks in summer, so for later colour try combining with a clematis such as *viticella* 'Blue Belle'.

Vigorous and very healthy, the arching stems making good spreading ground cover. The flowers are only slightly fragrant, but attractively shaped in dainty sprays that are very resistant to injury from wind or rain.

Red Blanket

A descendant of 'Yesterday', sharing its popular old-fashioned appearance and tough constitution, but with larger flowers, a slightly flat rosy red that stands out well against the dark foliage. As the name implies, excellent for covering large areas.

Season: Repeat flowering all summer.

Foliage: Glossy, dark green and shapely, almost evergreen, on vigorous arching growth.

Height: 75cm (2½ft)

Spread: 1.2–1.5m (4–5ft)

Soil: Most fertile, well-drained kinds.

Positioning: Full sun; as ground cover in larger beds and borders, and also for training on fences.

Care: Mulch beneath the trailing stems where possible in spring, and feed at mid-summer. Deadhead occasionally during summer.

Pruning: No special pruning needed, apart from an annual trim to shape in winter; reduce the height of vertical stems if necessary.

Useful tips: Try combining with 'Rosy Cushion' for effective companion planting. In many gardens its disease-resistance is still high, but some modern stocks show susceptibility to black spot, so watch out for this and spray if necessary.

Rosy Cushion

Season: Repeat flowering all summer.

Foliage: Dark green, glossy and plentiful.

Height: 75–90cm (2½–3ft)

Spread: 1.2–1.5m (4–5ft)

Soil: Fertile and well-drained.

Positioning: Full sun; as ground cover in larger beds and borders, as a specimen and for training on fences. Widely used by landscapers for massed planting in relatively inaccessible positions.

Care: Mulch in spring or feed at mid-summer. Deadhead occasionally during summer.

Pruning: Little needed. Trim to shape annually in winter and remove one or two old stems to encourage new growth.

Useful tips: An excellent choice for hiding drain covers, and also for covering banks. Its low spreading growth is an ideal support for a clematis such as 'Helios' or 'Gravetye Beauty'.

Another good rose bred from 'Yesterday', with bushy rounded growth that can be shaped to produce a weeping specimen for containers. The single blooms, loosely clustered with prominent gold stamens, have the dainty charm of a wild rose.

Season: Repeat flowering in summer.

Foliage: Large, deep green and prolific.

Height: 105cm (3½ft) or more

Spread: 90cm (3ft)

Soil: Any fertile, well-drained soil.

Positioning: Full sun or light shade; as specimens or in small groups in beds and borders; also as a climber.

Care: Manure in autumn and mulch in spring; feed in spring and again at mid-summer for good continuity.

Pruning: Hard pruning, cutting strong stems back by half, keeps plants bushy and well-flowering; may also be lightly pruned for larger shrubs, or trained and pruned as a short climber.

Useful tips: Try this one as a pillar rose, training it up to 1.8m (6ft) in a prominent position, or spread out the stems and tie them in evenly on horizontal wires to create a fan against a wall or fence.

Fragrance, flower form and good health are all strong features of this lovely rose. Although the blooms are large and fully rosette-shaped, the soft colouring creates an impression of delicacy and fragility.

Sally Holmes

Season: Repeat flowering all summer.
Foliage: Dark green and glossy.
Height: 1.5m (5ft)
Spread: 1.2m (4ft)
Soil: Rich and well-cultivated.
Positioning: Full sun with shelter from wind; as a specimen shrub in beds and borders, or in large containers.
Care: Manure in autumn and mulch in spring; water in dry seasons on lighter soils and feed at mid-summer.
Pruning: Shorten strong stems by one-third in winter and remove a few old branches annually from mature bushes to promote new growth.
Useful tips: Occasionally temperamental in a dull or cool summer. Vulnerable to wind damage, this makes a good choice for growing in a large tub in a sunny sheltered position; plant with summer climbers such as blue *Ipomoea* (Morning Glory) or scarlet *Eccremocarpus scaber* (Chilean Glory Vine).

In a slightly protected position this is an unusual and eye-catching rose, its large and persistent blooms held well above the foliage in loose conical bunches, so that the strong upright bushes seem to be studded with creamy white flower heads.

Scepter'd Isle

A new shrub rose of great charm, with short bushy growth that makes it ideal for the smaller garden. The best display of flowers, very full and fragrant, occurs early in the season; later blooms, while still attractive, have fewer petals.

Season: Repeat flowering all summer.

Foliage: Rich green, large and handsome.

Height: 75–90cm (2½–3ft)

Spread: 60cm (2ft)

Soil: Well-manured and deeply cultivated.

Positioning: Full sun; in small groups at the front of beds and borders, and as specimens in containers.

Care: Enjoys rich living, so manure well in autumn, mulch in spring and feed in spring and at mid-summer.

Pruning: Best pruned firmly in winter, taking strong stems down to half their height or even less to promote vigorous growth.

Useful tips: With its comparatively small size, may be grown singly in large pots, or three or four together as a group in a larger tub. Lavish a little extra care on maintaining good growing conditions for best results; may not repeat well in its first year.

Scharlachglut

Season: Early summer only.
Foliage: Large and dark green, on purple stems.
Height: 2.1–3m (7–10ft)
Spread: 1.8–2.1m (6–7ft)
Soil: Most kinds – tolerates poor soils.
Positioning: Full sun or light shade; as a specimen in large beds and borders, or in a woodland setting. The flower display is packed into comparatively few weeks but is quite spectacular, so try to provide a prominent position.
Care: Manure in autumn and mulch in spring; feed after flowering but do not deadhead.
Pruning: Shorten all long canes in winter by one third and cut out some of the old branches annually.
Useful tips: Try planting it as a climber, beside a small deciduous tree where some of the stems can scramble into the branches. To provide further colour when the short flowering season is over, plant a late-blooming clematis such as 'Ville de Lyon'.

A gorgeous and extrovert rose, also known as 'Scarlet Fire', with extremely vigorous and handsome growth. The very large single blooms are brilliant, with a clear central boss of stamens, and are followed by conspicuous urn-shaped orange hips.

A good fragrant white variety, almost apricot when the dense sprays of small flowers first open, with very vigorous tall shoots that help make it a dual-purpose rose: prune it as a large shrub or leave to reach full height as a rambler.

Season: Mainly early summer but repeats quite well.

Foliage: Bright green, medium-sized and well-spaced.

Height: 1.5m (5ft) or more

Spread: 1.2m (4ft)

Soil: Any fertile well-drained soil.

Positioning: Full sun or light shade; as a large specimen shrub in rose or mixed borders, or as a rambler.

Care: Mulch and feed in spring, and also manure in autumn on lighter soils. Tie in tall stems securely if grown as a rambler.

Pruning: Prune quite hard in winter, shortening strong stems by one-third, to maintain a large shrub; trim ramblers more lightly, removing some of the older stems when growth becomes too dense.

Useful tips: Perfect for training on arches and pergolas, where it will reach 2.4m (8ft) or more.

Suma

Season: Mid-summer and autumn.

Foliage: Reddish-green, turning crimson in autumn.

Height: 30–45cm (12–18in)

Spread: 90cm–1.2m (3–4ft)

Soil: Most kinds if fertile and well-drained.

Positioning: Full sun or light shade; as ground cover or edging; also in containers and grafted as a standard to provide colourful highlights at the corners of beds, in herb gardens for example.

Care: Manure in autumn and mulch in spring; feed after the first flush of blooms.

Pruning: Shorten some longer shoots in winter and remove one or two older stems to promote new growth.

Useful tips: Try this as a trailing plant for banks, raised beds and tall containers. May also be trained on walls or wire netting, fanning out the stems evenly to form a short climber. Even when out of flower, the foliage is very handsome.

A seedling from the well-known 'Nozomi', very low-growing although established bushes develop a neat hump of foliage in the centre. The arching stems are covered with clusters of small rosettes, especially attractive in autumn.

Descended from the well-known polyantha rose 'The Fairy', this tough hardy shrub thrives in a wide range of conditions and provides almost unbroken summer colour with its small 6cm (2½in) blooms evenly placed all over the branches.

Season:	Continuous all summer.
Foliage:	Small, dense and mid-green.
Height:	75–90cm (2½–3ft)
Spread:	1.2–1.5m (4–5ft)
Soil:	Fertile and well-drained.
Positioning:	Full sun or very light shade; as ground cover, edging or as a low hedge. Shrubby rather than prostrate, which increases its versatility, but in any position the dense growth is remarkably efficient at suppressing weeds.
Care:	Mulch in spring, and deadhead during summer. May need spraying with systemic fungicide in a poor summer.
Pruning:	Remove dead growth in winter, together with some of the older branches, and shorten excessively long young stems.
Useful tips:	A fine variety for large containers. One of a strong series of ground cover roses named after counties.

Season:	Repeat flowering all summer.
Foliage:	Glossy and rich green, with bronze tints.
Height:	45–60cm (18–24in)
Spread:	1.8m (6ft) in the best soils, but often less.
Soil:	Most kinds are suitable, if well-drained.
Positioning:	Full sun; as ground cover in larger beds and borders, on banks and in containers. Blooms are larger and more complex than most ground cover roses, so allow room for these to be displayed fully.
Care:	Manure in autumn and mulch in spring. Deadhead in summer.
Pruning:	No special pruning needed. Remove one or two old branches in winter and trim lightly to shape.
Useful tips:	A popular rose for large containers and for mixing with brightly coloured ground cover varieties. With its long season and heautiful blooms it is an inspired choice for window boxes.

Vigorous and wide spreading, valuable for covering large areas and also for its very full, prettily cupped double flowers gathered in large trusses. One of the best white ground cover roses and attractive in a wide range of positions.

Sweet Juliet

A robust full-leafed variety with a graceful upright habit that can be challenging to prune to shape: light trimming only is often favoured. Popular for its lovely pure apricot flowers that open from dainty buds.

Season: Early summer, but can repeat quite well.

Foliage: Light green, long and pointed.

Height: 1.2m (4ft)

Spread: 90cm (3ft)

Soil: Fertile and well-drained; tolerates poorer soils.

Positioning: Full sun, with plenty of space if you want a large shrub; grow as a specimen or in groups in larger borders. With their elegant and yet robust growth, three plants may be grouped together, 60cm (2ft) apart, to give the effect of a bold single shrub.

Care: Mulch and feed in spring; manure in autumn on poorer soils.

Pruning: Trim to shape in winter for large bushes, or prune harder, shortening strong stems by one-third, for better repeat flowering. Basal shoots may become congested and need thinning.

Useful tips: Give this variety time to build up into a strong bush when continuity of flowering will improve significantly.

The Dark Lady

Season: Repeat flowering all summer.

Foliage: Dark green and very large, on well-branched stems.

Height: 90cm (3ft)

Spread: 105cm (3½ft)

Soil: Most fertile well-drained soils are suitable.

Positioning: Full sun with plenty of space; as specimens in larger beds and borders. Its short stature makes this an ideal variety for massing in formal rose beds.

Care: Mulch and feed in spring and keep watered in dry seasons; manure poorer soils in autumn. Use a preventive spray routine against mildew.

Pruning: Best pruned fairly hard in winter, shortening most stems to half their height.

Useful tips: Plant this where the earlier flowers can be appreciated for their colour and fragrance. May be planted 60cm (2ft) apart to form a low hedge for edging paths and herbaceous borders.

Really deep red roses are always popular, and this one is stunning in early summer, its fragrant blooms opening quite flat and recurved, like a tree peony. Later blooms are still lovely, but slightly paler and less full.

Season: Early summer, and repeats quite well.

Foliage: Dark green, pointed and shapely.

Height: 60–75cm (2–2½ft)

Spread: 60–75cm (2–2½ft)

Soil: Rich with plenty of humus. Not a strong variety, so a very fertile soil is an essential prerequisite.

Positioning: Light shade; singly or in groups at the front of a bed or border; also in containers of all kinds.

Care: Manure well in autumn, mulch in spring, and feed in spring and at mid-summer; water in dry weather.

Pruning: Prune lightly, just removing dead wood and trimming to shape in winter.

Useful tips: Do not plant in bright sun as the blooms can scorch; needs good growing conditions to maintain disease resistance. Exploit its small size and arching habit by growing in large pots, and feed every 2–3 weeks for best results.

The beautifully formed small flowers, tightly packed with petals and gathered in attractive sprays, compensate for rather weak growth. Bushes have a low arching habit, presenting the fragrant rosettes perfectly in a front of border position.

Season: Repeats well from early summer.

Foliage: Mid-green, matt and well-formed.

Height: 1.2m (4ft)

Spread: 1.2m (4ft)

Soil: Fertile and well drained but will tolerate a wider range than many varieties

Positioning: Full sun or light shade; singly or in groups in large beds and borders, also excellent in containers.

Care: Very robust, so no special care needed beyond autumn manuring and a mulch of compost in spring.

Pruning: Prune lightly, thinning some of the twiggy growth in winter and shortening stronger stems to maintain a shapely bush.

Useful tips: Might need spraying against mildew, especially in a hot dry season. The similarity of habit between this variety, its sibling 'Redouté' and their common parent 'Mary Rose' is so great that all three could be combined in a single bed or border.

A sport from 'Mary Rose', with the same very tough constitution, although it can suffer a little from mildew. Flowering starts about a fortnight before many other varieties, and continues very regularly until autumn.

A versatile and popular rose that can be pruned and adapted for a number of different positions. Growth is compact and bushy, with graceful stems that are smothered with attractive foliage and very large clusters of small blooms that vary from pink to deep mauve.

Season:	Continuous all summer.
Foliage:	Small, dark green and shiny.
Height:	1.2m (4ft)
Spread:	1.2m (4ft)
Soil:	Most kinds if fertile and well-drained.
Positioning:	Full sun or light shade; as bedding or specimen plants, for hedging and also in containers; may be grafted on special rootstocks to produce decorative standards.
Care:	Manure in autumn and mulch in spring; feed at mid-summer in poorer soils.
Pruning:	Trim to shape in winter, and remove some of the old branches to stimulate new growth. May be pruned hard to reduce height as a ground cover rose.
Useful tips:	Plant 45cm (18in) apart for a dense flowering hedge. Blends into cottage garden schemes. Blooms well in large pots, where it will grow about half its normal size; feed every 2–3 weeks to sustain long flowering.